From My Heart To Yours

Don Tidwell

M.O.R.E. Publishers
Memphis, Tennessee

From My Heart To Yours

By Don Tidwell

Copyright 2019, by Don Tidwell
International Standard Book Number
(ISBN) 978-1-945344-11-4
Printed in the United States of America

M.O.R.E. Publishers

www.morepublishersstore.biz

Introduction
"From My Heart To Yours"
By Don Tidwell

My heart rejoices of the thought –
"the gift of love"
is what I'm saying.
We share the partnership with Jesus.
Put "Jesus Christ"
when you're praying.

We are servants of the work of Jesus.
In Heaven, Jesus will give us our Reward.
Jesus is the name of Eternal Life.
As servants, we are employed by the Lord.

When you feel life has let you down,
servants employed by Jesus have a
wonderful story.
Jesus is our love for eternal life.
Jesus will answer our prayers
to eternal glory.

Jesus is our life and love forever.
In our life, He brings us
happiness and cheer.
We walk with Jesus in our life.
What a joy it will be to share.
It would be nice to make this a reality.

With the love of Jesus, we will always care.
When your troubles arise,
that's when you go to Jesus in prayer.

The doors of Heaven are open.
He lets us see what is beyond
for this is our life forever.
Living here on earth is done.

A DREAM

Last night I had a dream
that Jesus was talking to me.
He said, "Someday I'm coming back.
That, I want you to believe."

Jesus said, "My sheep have gone astray.
Not all! Some still believe.
That glorious day when I return,
I'll carry them home safely with me.

I hear your prayers every day.
I answer each and every one.
When I return to receive you as my own,
then your life will have just begun.

There will be no pain or sorrow.
Life will be happy an carefree.
You will again walk with the ones you love -
here in Heaven - for eternity.
(Don Tidwell)

A GREAT MAN

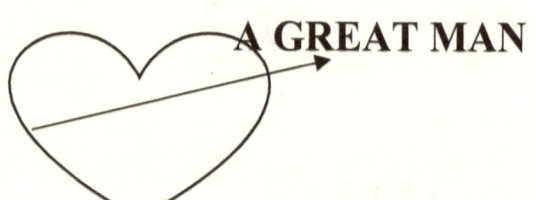

This great man is growing old
forgetting the machinery and the noise.
It's time for him to enjoy life
with his four girls and boys.

A great man has a great outlook on life
without a worry on his mind
with wrinkles on his face and hands
no other man is so kind.

He talks with words so soft and kind
as gentle as the wind can blow.
He's also loved by everyone -
this man with hair white as snow.

This man I have loved all my life;
to lose him would be so sad.
He's not just an ordinary man.
This Great Man is My Dad.

(Don Tidwell)

A LETTER

Today, I received a letter
from someone I didn't know.
Opening the letter to see what it said,
this is the way it read.

"Sir, you don't know me.
As you read on you will find,
the one I'm writing to you about
once belonged to you; she's now mine.

In her sleep she calls your name
as tears roll down her eyes.
To know she still loves you -
it hurts when she cries.

She calls your name so softly
as her arms begin to reach.
For it's you who's in her dreams
that makes her cry in her sleep."
(Don Tidwell)

A LOVE WORTH REMEMBERING

A lesson earned, is a lesson learned.
To forget you seems afar.
Not only did you break my heart;
you left me with a scar.

The day when you walked away
the door of my heart you left ajar.
Memories are not all you left behind.
You left me with a scar.

A scar you left on my heart
cut deeply, like a knife.
One that will follow me forever
as it becomes a part of my life.

Someone else was in your life.
I couldn't seem to get through.
If he decides he doesn't want you,
always remember "I do".

(Don Tidwell)

A MOTHER'S LOVE

From the day you were conceived
in your mother's womb,
you were loved, cherished, and protected
waiting for the flower to bloom.

Each day her love grew deeper
as the baby began to grow;
waiting for that final hour
to introduce it to the world we know.

As she holds you in her arms
with those baby cries;
you are a part of her body -
the love you can see in her eyes.

With thanks, we give to Jesus -
sent from Heaven above.
There's no greater joy in living,
than a Mother's love.
(Don Tidwell)

←——————————————→

A PRESENT

I sit there thinking of you
about the good times we had together,
we made it through all the bad times
through all kinds of weather.

I awake in the mornings.
Sometimes I want to cry.
The beautiful love God has given us
shows love is a present, money can't buy.

A present that is given freely;
a love so faithful and kind;
I thank Jesus all the time
that you belong to me and you're mine.

Without you,
my life would be incomplete.
I work really hard to try.

Losing you would be a loss.
Love is a present, money can't buy.

I thank Jesus every night and day..
In our heart, there will be no goodbye.
In Jesus' hands, He holds us together.
Love is a present, money can't buy.

(Don Tidwell)

A SHADOW OF YOU

What I would give
just for a shadow of you;
to walk beside me in the moonlight,
the sunlight,
in the morning dew?

I would give everything in a lifetime
just for a shadow of you
to walk beside me in the moonlight,
the sunlight,
in the morning dew.

I would give me a stairway to Heaven
just for a shadow of you
to walk beside me in the moonlight,
the sunlight,
in the morning dew.

I have one thing left to offer.

My life, I would give to you
to walk beside me in the moonlight,
the sunlight,
in the morning dew.
(Don Tidwell)

ARMS OF AN ANGEL

When I gave my heart to Jesus
I prayed others will do the same.
Their life would be changed forever
as we pray these words in Jesus' Name.

Jesus answers all our prayers -
a story I had to tell.
They wonder why I'm always happy.
I'm in the arms of an angel.

I talk to Jesus before I sleep at night,
that all will be happy and well.
When I am awakened in the morning;
sleeping in the arms of an angel.

As we pray for our world today,
we look at every angel.
Our rest will be so peaceful,
sleeping in the arms of an angel.

When we accept Jesus in our life
we know we will never fail.
Jesus walks beside us step by step
in the arms of an angel.

(Don Tidwell)
Art by Melvin UpChurch ©M.O.R.E. Publishers

BLOWING KISSES IN THE WIND

When my little girl was three -
this is where it all began.
I would look at her and say,
"Daddy," while blowing kisses in the wind.

While other children were playing,
she would stay inside with me.
as I have said before,
my little girl is only three.

Now that she has gotten older -
her age now is ten.
She would look at me and say,
"Daddy, I'm blowing kisses in the wind."

One day while playing outside,
she looked up at me to say,
"Daddy, I am getting older.
I'll have to stop going out to play."

One day Jesus called her home.
I pray that my broken heart will mend.
I can still hear her say
"Daddy, I am blowing kisses in the wind."
(Don Tidwell)

HAND FULL OF LOVE

From the day you were born -
sent from Heaven above;
loaned to me by Jesus, to call my own,
I called you, my hand full of love.

As I held you in my arms,
my love surrounds you like a glove.
As we grew together, my pet name for you
was Hand Full of Love.

From day to day I watched you grow.
We joked of my pet name for you.
We laughed.
We cried.
We were as one.
Without you, what would I do?

We shared laughter,
conversations,
and silence.
Our thoughts were the same.

My love for you grew deeper
as Hand Full of Love became your name.

Then one day Jesus called him home.
His eyes closed like the wings of a dove.
I saw him smile. I heard his whisper,
"Daddy,
I'll always be your Hand Full of Love."
(Don Tidwell)

HEAVEN IS HOME

When you look up at the sky,
as you stare into space,
can you even imagine "Heaven"
as such a beautiful place?

On bending knees with your head bowed,
as you talk to Jesus in prayer,
have you thought about the hereafter -
a beautiful place? I want to go there.

Your friends and family are waiting
as you walk up to those Golden Gates.
There Jesus will place judgement upon you.
You will see your love, your family, your
mate.

as you walk inside those Golden Gates
the smile you will see on their face;
your family's arms, reaching out for you,
at home in Heaven -
such a beautiful place.

(Don Tidwell)

I DON'T EVEN KNOW HER NAME

While taking my early morning walk
I passed by a house today.
A little girl was playing.
She didn't see me walk away.

The next morning taking my walk,
this little girl was playing a game.
She looked up and call me Daddy,
and I don't even know her name.

I asked Jesus why she called me daddy
as I said my prayers today.
She still crosses my mind
and why this little girl talked this way.

Maybe something happened to her parents
and I can't help her with the pain.
This little girl called me daddy
and I don't even know her name.

(Don Tidwell)

I JUST NEED TO TALK

Mom, why don't you listen?

Something is on my mind.
I need someone to talk to.
Would you please be so kind?

I'm not a child anymore.
I also have problems too.

Why don't you listen, Mom?

You said, always come to you.

Please Mom, don't shut me out.
Don't make me walk.
I'm only just a teenager.
I just need to talk.

I feel like I'm being trapped
and I've just been caught.
I wish you would have listened Mom.

I just needed to talk.
(Don Tidwell)

I WANNA LIVE!!!

There will always be
troubles in our world.

Things happen
that we don't understand.

When it comes to an innocent child,
I will always be their biggest fan.

I don't know
why women get an abortion.

This child has a heartbeat.
Don't women have a since of pride?
Their master, they will have to meet.

A child should be heard not hurt.

This is only an opinionated option.
Most women would love a child.
Why not put the baby up for adoption.

What?
I'm thinking it could be wrong.

To me,
it's murder whatever they do.
Yet,
you can't only just blame the woman.
You have to blame the doctor too.

I wish abortions were never allowed.
I'm trying to put this mild.
How could just any woman?
How could they murder their child?
(Don Tidwell)

IF ONLY

If only I had one second that you didn't cross
my mind.
It would be a joyous reunion
of this thing we call "Mother" to me.

Maybe I could go in another second.
This would give me two.
One to relieve my mind of this pressure,
and two, I could stop thinking of you.

If only I could gain a day - a few seconds at
a time.
My life would be fulfilled again,
to clear you of my mind.

Each second would be another day.
My memories of you would end.
Each day would be a lifetime,
and I could live again.

Each day would be rewarding,
and I wouldn't be so lonely.
I could give my heart to another.
Then life would begin, "IF ONLY".

(Don Tidwell)

JESUS ANSWERED PRAYERS

It was just an ordinary day.

Troubles had filled my mind.
A knock at my door;
a friend stood there.
"Mother wishes to see you,
if you have time."

As I hurried to reach her home,
the door opened.
I entered there.

Her feeble arms and hands reached for me.
She looked at me and said,
"I need your prayer."

I asked,
"Of all the friends you have,
why am I the chosen one?"

She replied, "I've seen Jesus in you
and all the good you have done."

"I need for you to pray for me.
I haven't long here to stay."

I accepted her feeble hands,
and on my knees,
I began to pray.

I prayed for Jesus to take her home.
She was ready and didn't want to stay.
As I prayed at this woman's bedside,
I felt her life slip away.

(Don Tidwell)

JUST A PICTURE ON THE WALL

I've often wondered,
what went wrong,
as I walk down the hall.

If I could only focus straight ahead,
and keep my eyes off the picture on the wall.

My friends say I will be alright.

They would be so appalled,
if I would remove
the picture
that I have hanging on the wall.

The picture keeps me wanting to live;
reminding of a beautiful love I recall.

It will always be in my memory -
just a picture on the wall.

Time for bed.
I turn on the night light
so I won't stumble and fall.

However,
it's just an excuse,
to see the picture - just a picture on the wall.
(Don Tidwell)

JUST THE MEMORY

The days have come and gone
and I thought only of myself.
All I want is just the memory.
You can have all that is left.

As I look around for you,
our home was the home base.
I can see you clearly in the light
when I look and see your face.

Material things mean nothing.
My love for you will always be kept.
All I want is just the memory.
You can have all that's left.

I think about you all the time.
Willingly, I have no choice.
I can hear you say, "I love you,"
with that beautiful, lovely voice.

I must go on and find myself
the beautiful love that I have felt.
All I want is just the memory.
You can have all that's left.

(Don Tidwell)

LIFE WITHOUT PAROLE

Nothing is more loving than Jesus.
We think we are in control.
He held me in his loving arms and gave me
life without Parole.

They say you might see Jesus
and Heaven's such a lovely place.
You might even see a smile
when you look upon Jesus' Face.

As we walked to the Golden Gates
I knew I had reached my goal.
He held me in his loving arms
and gave me life without Parole.

I could see Jesus at the Golden Gates.
And for the beautiful things I see,
I'm so thankful to Jesus
that my Jesus has chosen me.

Don't give up on Jesus,
and of stories we have been told.
He held me in his loving arms
and gave me life without Parole.

(Don Tidwell)

LITTLE TOMMY

While taking a walk in the park,
to a little boy
whose face was so dear,
I asked him simply,
"Is everything OK?"

"Yes," he replied.
"Little Tommy meets me here."

I asked who was Little Tommy?

He looked at me with a face so kind.
"Little Tommy has always been my friend
because Little Tommy is blind."

"Kids would laugh as he held my arm
as we walked through the park.
They just don't understand.
Little Tommy walks in the dark."

As I returned from my walk,
the little boy was still standing there.
Then as I walked up to help him,
at a special house he would stare.

As I knocked,
the door opened wide.

A lady appeared,
and I knew something was wrong.

She asked me to tell the little boy waiting
that "Little Tommy has passed on."
(Don Tidwell)

LOVE
DOESN'T LIVE HERE ANY MORE

The day you walked out of my life,
we were happy as can be.
I don't understand what went wrong.
Trouble was coming that I couldn't see.

As I awakened this morning
remembering,
last night was just like before.

My friends all ask about you,
and I tell them
"Love doesn't live here anymore."

Public Domain Photo

Love doesn't live here anymore.
Yet, I don't remember crossing the floor.
I can hardly remember my name,
now that love doesn't live here anymore.

You said that you loved me,
many times, as before.
I wish I had an answer why
"Love doesn't live here anymore."
(Don Tidwell)

MEMORIES OF THE PAST

My wife of many years;
her heart made of Gold;
she has to love me from the heart
of a story to be told.

Memories are things in the past
of a thin drawn line.
I know beyond a doubt,
you love me with a love so kind.

A home? My mind filled with thoughts
of a memory of the past
where with one there were no boundaries
of a love that didn't last.

Her loving arms embrace me
as she walks up from behind.
Her words so softly spoken,
"I understand dear,
she just crossed your mind."
(Don Tidwell)

MY BEDTIME PARTNER AND ME

When I lay on my bed to sleep
and my bedtime partner holds me tight,
I couldn't live without my bedtime Partner
I just couldn't sleep at night.

As I put my arms around my bedtime
Partner and my eyes begin to close,
my bedtime Partner is there for me.
It's like a beautiful Red Rose.

It's just a comfort to know
my bedtime Partner is there for me.
As I awake in the morning time
I read each chapter carefully.

As I read each chapter one by one,
my bedtime Partner gives me a test.
That's why I sleep good at night
whenever I lay down to rest.

Photo by Colin Carey

Jesus puts his arms around me
as I go through the day.
My Bible is my bedtime Partner.
That's why I feel this way!!!
(Don Tidwell)

MY HAPPINESS

When Jesus had taken her from me
in my heart I was truly blessed.
Yet, I don't understand why
Jesus could take away my happiness.

We loved each other with a passion
and we knew it came from above.
He gave me a wonderful woman
that I would always love.

My love, I know you're in Heaven.
Sometimes, I just can't see
why Jesus took away my happiness.
He's the one who gave you to me.

We don't know when Jesus is ready.
A lot of things we have said.
When Jesus took away my happiness
why couldn't he have taken me instead?

Jesus knows what's best for me
and I know I must confess,
I really don't understand why
Jesus took away my happiness.
(Don Tidwell)

NO TEARDROPS IN HEAVEN

As you enter into the Lord's Temple
your eyes will open wide.
There will be no teardrops in Heaven.
We have nothing to hide.

All we have to do is have Faith.
We put our troubles in Jesus Hands.
He will lead us all to Victory
where it all began.

Jesus will walk with us step by step.
All you will see is a grin.
There will be no teardrops in Heaven
and our broken hearts will mend.

There will be no sin in Heaven,
with the Angels flying by.
There will be no teardrops in Heaven.
That's why you will never cry.

You will look and grin at Jesus
and a smile will be on his Face.
There will be no teardrops in Heaven
and there will be nothing left to waste.

(Don Tidwell)

ONE SHE CAN'T FORGET

The day she walked away,
she thought there would be no pain.
But her heart seems to break in two
at the sound of his name.

By chance or by faith,
she knew this wasn't a game.
If you want to see her cry,
just call out his name.

Her face, a blank expression
as tears begin to fall.
Just the mention of his name
makes her bounce off the wall.

As days turn into years
and nothing seems to change,
her eyes still fill with tears
at the mention of his name.

(Don Tidwell)

ONE YOU LEFT BEHIND

Dear, you left me alone today
in this world you and I called home;
with these memories in my mind,
I'm the one you left behind.

I ask myself why me?
The answer I couldn't find.
Then the memories surround me, reminding
me, I'm the one you left behind.

Did you have to go so soon?
We never had a chance at life.
Then the memories surround me, reminding
me, you were my loving wife.

Now I share this world alone
with these memories in my mind,
of all the love we once shared
and remembering,
I'm the one you left behind.

(Don Tidwell)

ONLY JUST A MEMORY

I remember when she walked away.
I thought I would forget in time.
Many years have come and gone
and today, she's still on my mind.

I think about the love we had.
Memories of her I want to share.
I think of her quite often because you see,
I still care.

I wish she would return to me;
a chance I wish she would take
because now when she crosses my mind,
I can feel my heart begin to break.

Sometimes strange things may happen.
I know it's hard to believe.
Now, she has left me behind
with only, just a memory.
(Don Tidwell)

OUR LAST SUNSET

While growing up as a child
it was hard for me to believe.

My growing up throughout childhood,
Jesus was always there for me.

He allowed Linda to walk into my life.

There was the beautiful time
when we first met;
the love we shared
was so beautiful because
she always loved to watch the sunset.

Later in the evening time
you could always bet,
Linda was ready to go outside
for she smiled at the sunset.

Jesus gave us to each other and
a smile as we looked at each other's face.

What more could we ask for,
while sitting here in this beautiful place?

Jesus was ready for her to come home.

In my heart I will never forget,
the love we shared for each other
"Not Knowing" it was our last sunset.
(Don Tidwell)

Public Domain Photo

OUR LOVE IS BEYOND REPAIR

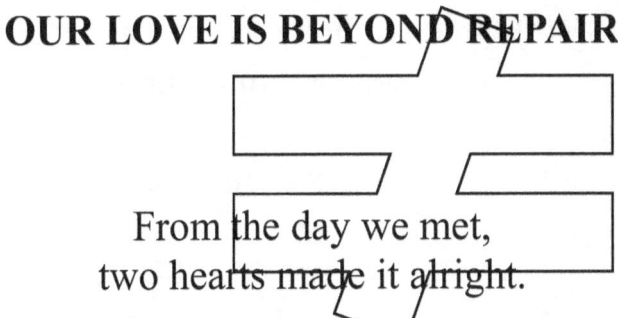

From the day we met,
two hearts made it alright.

We gave each other happiness
and the moon was shining bright.

Now it's time to bring out the truth
and I know it doesn't seem fair
to know our love is dying.

Our love is beyond repair.

I hope someday you will find
what you're looking for and more.

I hope that you will be happy
watching me walk out the door.

It's hard to understand why
for me your love doesn't care.

Now that we have walked away
our love is beyond repair.

People were always seeing us together.

Now they just stop and stare.
I just tell them "It's all over."

Our love is beyond repair.
(Don Tidwell)

PICTURE OF YOU IN MY MIND

www.pexels.com

I remember the day we met!

On your face a smile began to appear.
I could tell you felt the same -
the love we would hold so dear.

You gave me more happiness.

You gave me all you could give.
Just knowing you were at my side,
It gave me a reason to live.

When I awake in the morning,
my love is a thin-drawn line.
Now all I have left
is a picture of you in my mind.

When we shared our love together
our love for each other was fine.
Now all that I have left
is a picture of you in my mind.

I know you have found someone new.

It seems that I'm in a bind.
Now all I have left,
is a picture of you in my mind.
(Don Tidwell)

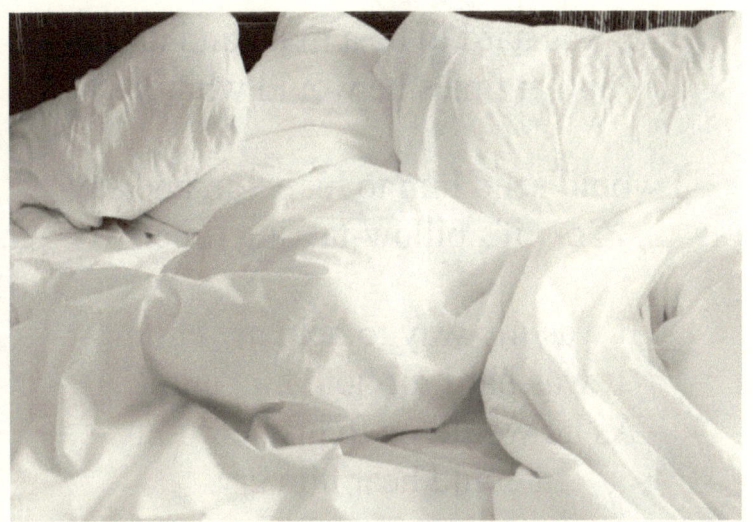

Photo by Jaymantri (www.pexels.com)

PILLOW TALKING TIME

Growing up at an early age
was hard for my little boy.

I was his life, mom, and dad.
He was such a great joy.

Living a life was such great fun as a family.
We had a beautiful life.
One day Jesus called her home.
My son lost a Mother.
I lost a wife.

It was hard to be a mom and dad
and at times he would whine.

I would send him to his room and say
"Son, it's pillow-talking time."

It was my way to help my child.
It was hard for both him and I.
As he would go to his bedroom,
I could hear him cry.

As he would talk to his pillow
I could hear him as he began to weep.

Jesus would close his eyes
and my little boy would sleep.
(Don Tidwell)

POWER OF JESUS

Today, my heart is weary and sad
as my son lay on the bed
with tubes down his mouth and nose;
not knowing if alive or dead.

A kidney donor was needed desperately
if my son was to live.

I prayed to Jesus,
"Give my son life, in Jesus Name,
if it be Thou will."

I could feel the power of Jesus
more powerful than before.

As I prayed at my son's bedside,
a stranger crossed the floor.

His arms reached out to comfort my pain.

He whispered,
"Jesus said,
it will be fine;

to tell you to look no more;
that your child
is welcome to one of mine."
(Don Tidwell)

RESERVED SEAT IN HEAVEN

Jesus asked me to come home
and he asked me for my hand.

As I arose to accept him,
Jesus carried me to the promise land.

He told me about the seats in Heaven.
I pray one of them is for me.

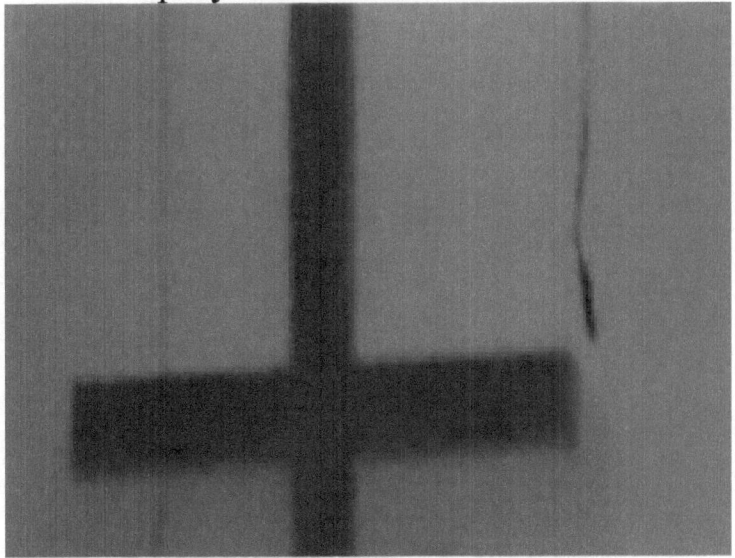

Jesus looked at me and smiled,

"Yes, there is one for thee."

I have no fear of dying.

My soul will always be clear.
I have a reserved seat in Heaven.
So, there is nothing left to fear.

When I go to rest at night,
I pray Jesus will come for me
to see my reserved seat in Heaven;
what a beautiful place to see.

That lovely day when Jesus comes;
the days of the week are seven.
I'll have myself a smile on my face.
I'll get to see my reserved seat in Heaven.

(Don Tidwell)

SAYING GOODBYE

God has a plan as we grow.

Things turn around what we call life.
God joins together man and woman
that we call man and wife.

Days turn into years,
and time keeps going on.
For some reason we fall apart.
We wonder what went wrong.

One heart will be broken.
The other will hold a smile.

One doesn't want to be together.
Let's just say, we call this style.

Years later down the road,
you feel you were denied.
You are trying to say "Hello" again
but this time,
I am saying "Goodbye."
(Don Tidwell)

SOMEBODY TO SOMEONE

Many months we've been together.
Now it all has come undone.
You choose to live without me;
but tonight,
I'll be somebody to someone.

As I lay here in her arms,
it's just a game of fun.
For tonight I'll remember,
I'll be somebody to someone.

It's not the love we once had.
She's not the chosen one.
Yet as we lay beside each other tonight,
I'll be somebody to someone.

It's not you
here in my arms.
I gave you my
all above and beyond.
But just for tonight,
I'll be somebody to someone.

(Don Tidwell)

This Photo by Unknown Author is licensed under CC BY-SA

STREETS PAVED WITH GOLD

When Jesus accepts me as his own,
and my life begins to unfold,
I want to go to that place in Heaven
where the streets are paved with Gold.

Yes, I want to go to that City
where life is happy and carefree.
It's a life that Jesus gave me.
That's where I want to be.

I want to see this Place called Heaven
and I will hold Myself liable;
building my trust in Jesus,
as I sit and read my Bible.

Jesus will sit down beside me.

If I may seem so bold,
I want to see this place called Heaven
where the streets are paved with Gold.

Jesus, I need your help for me.
I pray that His arms shall open
for me to hold.
I want to see this place called Heaven,
where the streets are paved with Gold.

(Don Tidwell)

TATTERED AND TORN

An old man came to
church today.
His clothes were
faded
and well worn.
His face was kind
and held a smile
that said,
"I'm like my Bible.
          I'm tattered and torn."

He said, "I came to talk to Jesus.
I'm getting on in years."

And as he spoke, he talked with pride.
I could feel my eyes swelling with tears.

My life has had its ups and downs.
When I go home,
there's no one to morn.
My Bible is my pathway to Heaven
even though it's tattered and torn.

After worship service he slipped away.
My thoughts of him still fresh in my mind,
I prayed to Jesus, "Please let me find him
so, I can talk to him one more time."

As I arrived at his home that day,
He was in Heaven with no one to morn.
In his hands he held a Bible -
a Bible tattered and torn.
(Don Tidwell)

Hamilton Chapel Photo

THE GRASS NEEDS THE RAIN

When you made up your mind to leave
I knew it would never be the same.
In my heart I really need you
like the grass needs the rain.

Do you sometimes think of me;
the beautiful things we have done?
Jesus put us together for a reason
because you were my chosen one.

How can you just walk away?
To try and forget would be so sad;
a beautiful love, a beautiful happiness,
and the love we once had.

As I sit here trying to forget
I know this is not a game,
and my heart really needs you
like the grass needs the rain.

I know I had a part in your leaving.
I can't let you take all the blame.
I want you to know, my heart needs you,
like the grass needs the rain.

(Don Tidwell)

THE IMPORTANCE OF MAMA

As a child, we never realize
Mama gave us a shoulder to cry on.
Mama was always there for me.
I really miss her, now she's gone.

As a child, you skinned your knee.
Mama's love was always true.
It didn't matter -right or wrong –
Mama was always there for you.

I know Mama is beside Jesus.
My love for her is so divine.
But the importance of Mama
will never leave my mind.

If I could change things in my life,
I would put Mama Number One.
If only I could see her smile at me,
the importance of Mama would be done.

Now that we have gotten older
we now have children of our own.
We never knew
how much Mama would be missed.

The importance of Mama - Jesus took home.
(Don Tidwell)

https://free-images.com

THE MAN ON THE CROSS

The beauty of the sun as it rises
and the lives that have been lost;
we wonder what we could change
when we remember the man on the Cross.

He gave us many things to do.
Sometimes we feel like an outcast.
Just keep believing in Jesus
and forget about the past.

Don't forget to remind others,
Jesus will be with us at all cost.
He loves us each the same
and always remember the one on the Cross.

We sleep at night and forget to pray;
to thank Jesus for what he has done.
He gave us happiness in our life.
Always put Jesus Number one.

Think about the love He gave us.
Jesus will always be the boss.
Remember Jesus loves us dearly
and remember the man on the Cross.
(Don Tidwell)

https://free-images.com

THE OLD ROCKING CHAIR

It was early in the morning
when a friend came into my mind.
He had given me an album of Mama's
pictures I thought I would never find.

Mama had always been there for me.
So, memories of her I want to share
for as a child, I never realized
the beauty of the Old Rocking Chair.

On the front porch Mama was rocking
and I couldn't help but weep.

It was me, in her arms.
She was rocking me to sleep.

The memories came flooding back
seeing the early morning
and Mama sitting there;
holding her baby,
rocking back and forth,
in her Old Rocking Chair.

Mama I know you are with Jesus.

The place on the porch is bare.
I still picture Mama in my mind,
rocking in her Old Rocking Chair.
(Don Tidwell)

THE ONE ON THE CROSS

The beauty
of the sun rises.

And because of the lives
that have been lost,
we wonder what we could change
as we remember The One on The Cross.

He gave us a lot of things to do.
Sometimes we feel like an outcast.
Just keep believing in Jesus,
and forget about the past.

Don't forget to remind others
Jesus is with them at all cost.
He loves us each the same -
Yes, that's The One on The Cross.

We sleep at night and forget to pray;
to thank Jesus for what he has done.
He gave us
happiness in our life.

So always put Jesus Number One.

Remember the love he's given us.
Jesus will always be the boss.
Jesus loves us dearly,
So, remember "The One On The Cross".
(Don Tidwell)

THROW AWAY HER MEMORY

I want to live a long time
and it's hard to believe
I have to throw away her memory
before her memory kills me.

Many nights, I walk the floor
trying to get her off my mind.
It seems impossible to forget her.
My friends say it takes time.

I have all the time in the world
trying hard to go on you see.
I have to throw away her memory
before her memory kills me.

Every day I walk around in a daze;
if only I could let it be.
I have to throw away her memory
before her memory kills me.

(Don Tidwell)

TOO BLESSED TO BE STRESSED

It had taken me a lifetime.
Now I have to confess,
while growing up to middle age
I didn't give Jesus my best.

A new beginning was coming my way
when I gave Jesus my heart.
Jesus gave me a reason to smile again.
I was a work of art.

I look at the world in a different way.
My life was changing for the best.
Now that Jesus came into my life,
I'm too blessed to be stressed.

I've been through trial and error.
My life was just a stage.
I asked Jesus for his blessings.
Now I have to turn the page.

My life has had its ups and downs.
It was only just a test.
I asked Jesus for his blessings.
Now I'm too blessed to be stressed.
(Don Tidwell)

TROUBLED HEART

I awakened early this morning.
Troubles were here to stay.
How can I face tomorrow?
I can't face today.

I look up to Heaven.
Lord, help me I pray.
How can I face tomorrow?
I can't face today.

The moon lights up the night
and my mind goes astray.
How can I face tomorrow?
I can't face today.

Salvation came into my heart.
My troubles vanished away.
Now, I can face tomorrow.
Jesus, helped me face today.
(Don Tidwell)

WHEN HE'S READY FOR YOU

When you look out your window
and the morning light is breaking through,
are you ready for Jesus,
when he's ready for you?

The life we have been living
doesn't seem so happy and carefree.
Since Jesus entered my body,
I know he loves you and me.

When you look up to Heaven
the sky you see is blue.
Are you ready for Jesus
when he's ready for you?

When you're ready to question your mind
and the angels are flying near,
then you know Jesus is coming.
In your heart there is nothing to fear.

As you get on your knees to pray,
It's the best thing we can do.
For are you ready for Jesus
when he's ready for you?
(Don Tidwell)

While staring out my window
I thought about our life.
Jesus gave my son a wonderful Mommy.
He gave me a wonderful wife.

Today my son came up to me.
He looked so lost and alone.
Tears rolling down his cheeks he asked,
"Daddy, when is Mommy coming home?"

How do you tell a child,
at the golden age of four,
Jesus has taken his Mommy home.
She won't be coming back anymore.

It breaks my heart,
to see my son cry.
But we know life must go on.
Still my child looked up to me and asked,
"Daddy, when is Mommy coming home?"

Our life will have to change.
In Jesus Name we will belong.
But I will have the answer
when my child looks up at me and ask,
"Daddy, when is Mommy coming home?"
(Don Tidwell)

WHEN JESUS
COMES FOR YOU

The days are going by so fast.
We wonder,
"What should we do?"

We can't change the hands of time.
What will you do
when Jesus comes for you?

He will give you
all the happiness;
will also give you a new start.

You won't have
any enemies
with his love in your heart.

When Jesus
talks to you at night,
as you sit down to say a prayer,
our enemies
will be our friends.
Jesus will always be there.

Jesus is
the love of our life;
the feeling of our heart goes through.
You will walk down that Golden Path.

What
will you
do,
When
Jesus
comes
for you?

You can
feel his
hands
as they
touch
your
face.

I am ready Jesus, to walk with you.
Are you ready for it all?
What will you do,
when Jesus comes for you?
(Don Tidwell)

WHEN LOVE IS COMPLETE

Today while walking in the park,
an older couple sat there talking.
Eaves dropping was not my specialty,
but I had to stop walking.

He said, "Through all the laughter and tears,
as gray has touched your hair,
I found myself still smiling.
I couldn't help but stare.

Though the wrinkles have touched your face
and age has taken its toll,
when happy times go by so fast,
our bodies are growing old."

He touched her hand with loving care -
the love glowed on his face.
He smiled and looked into her eyes
and he told her, she couldn't be replaced.

"If I could live my life over again,
after all we've been through,
There is nothing I would change,
I would still want to share it with you."
(Don Tidwell)

WITNESS TO A PRAYER

I awakened early this Sunday Morning
to another beautiful day.
"What can I do for you Jesus?" I asked.
Then I began to pray.

On my way to the morning service,
a little boy sat under a tree.
With a sad look across his face,
He asked, "Mister will you talk with me?"

It wasn't just another morning.
Jesus had a change in plan.
On my way to morning worship,
I was to witness to this little man.

Many years have come and gone
of that special day.
This is the first time in his life,
I had heard that little boy pray.

As I accepted the Pastor's hand,
he smiled and said,
"You don't remember me?
Think back many years ago,
I'm that little boy who sat under the tree."
(Don Tidwell)

YELLOW ROSE

Mother never had much in life
and then her time arose.
God had given her a child and more.
It was going to be her yellow rose.

Mother would look out of her window;
on her face would be a smile.
Happiness was in her life.
Playing outside was her child.

Sometimes Mother would go hungry.
This is where it all goes -
making sure her family had plenty.
That was Mother's Yellow Rose

Sometimes we never look ahead.
We miss seeing life as it glows.
We always thought about mother.
She always loved the Yellow Rose.

Now that we have gotten older,
living our life that we chose,
after seeing what Mother had given -
we know we were Mother's Yellow Rose.
(Don Tidwell)

INDEX